*A FLAME THAT NEVER DIES*

**Kindling the Flame**

**Igniting the Fire Within**

By: **Tonya Stewart**

*HOW TO KEEP THE FIRE BURNING*

*IN YOUR*

*PERSONAL RELATIONSHIP*

*WITH GOD*

## *DEDICATION*

Thank you Jesus for interceding that my faith fails not to write the vision and make it plain. This book is dedicated to My heavenly Father who has afforded me the opportunity to birth out this book. To My earthly father and mother Elder Alex Griffin and Georgia Griffin who has been a great inspiration to me along my journey. Through many great trials and tests he ordained for me to come out triumphantly. To my husband Pastor Kenneth Stewart who has stood by my side through thick and thin. I love you Babe. To our children Kayla and Kenny G who we know the perfect will of God will be accomplished in your lives. Honor to one of my spiritual mothers in the ministry Pastor Shirley Deavens, for the wisdom, inspiration, courage and knowledge imparted in me. Also to my spiritual daughter Elder Larita Rice for helping me birth the first book of many to come for in the Kingdom of God.

Last but definitely not least to the World Overcomers Christian Center Fellowship Family, I love you with all my heart. To every Preacher, Teacher, Pastor, Apostle, Prophet, Elder and member May God continue to richly bless you. To all Let the Light Shine, Let It Shine…

## *SPECIAL THANKS*

To all of those who have prayed for me, imparted life to me,

May God grant Grace and Favor upon your lives.

## Content

## *Introduction*

Kindle the fire within by Keeping the fire burning requires fanning the flame and the torch will remain lit. After all Kindle means to start (a fire); cause (a flame, blaze) to begin burning. How many believers today wake up every day to start a fire by sharing the Word of God with other people in the world that will ignite the gifts and talents that have been preordained by God for believers and Christians to use for the Kingdom so God is glorified?

**Chapter 1**

**Let the fire keep on burning within**

When we think about the word fire we automatically

visualize something hot. Yet, fire consists of flames with

multiple colors.  However, God is the consuming fire who

comes to consume strongholds that are setup by the enemy

to devastate the lives of believers. As we look at the life of

Moses in Ex. 3:2, 3 says, And the Angel of the Lord

appeared to him in a flame of fire from the midst of a bush.

So he looked and behold the bush was burning with fire,

but the bush was not consumed. So Moses had a

supernatural visitation from God. The flame represented the

Shekinah glory. God manifested Himself in various forms

of fire on many different occasions to get our attention. We find God manifesting himself as a pillar of fire (Exodus 13:21). We find God in the flame on the altar (Judg. 13:20). We come to the conclusion that God is the one who answers by fire. Yet Jer. 20: 9 describes God word in his heart to be like a burning fire shut up in his bones. So we now realize that fire can be viewed in several and different kinds of components. The fire keeps burning in believers when he or she realizes who lives   inside their temple. What is a temple? It is a place of worship or sanctuary. First of all we want to establish in our case 1Cor. 3:16 oppose to us a fact in a question format. Do you not know that you are the temple of God and that the Spirit of God dwells in you?  God dwells among believers by his Holy Spirit. Every Christian is a living temple of the living God.

Christ by his Spirit dwells in all believers who have received him as Savior. The physical temples and Christians were set apart for the service of God. They are sacred to him. Christians are holy by profession, and should be pure and clean both in heart and conversation. We need to know that our body is the temple of the Holy Spirit and we don't belong to ourselves because we have been bought with a price and Jesus Christ is the one who paid for our sins on the Cross. In 1 Cor. 3:17 If anyone defiles the temple of God, God will destroy him. For the temple of God is holy which temple are you holy our unholy? We belong to God and when we use our bodies or temples in the wrong manner there will be consequences. When people eat the wrong food what happens? High blood pressure, Diabetes, and High Cholesterol are the consequences of eating the wrong foods. However, people use their vessels for their own pleasures and self- gain as a result they receive sicknesses like Aids, herpes and HIV. Therefore, for this very reason believers have to keep on burning the fire within. We have to understand the fact that God is our Jehovah Mekadish- the sanctifier of our soul. In the book 2 Chronicles in Chapter 7:1-3 We find a man named Solomon who teaches us how to let the fire keep on burning in the temples. The bible says When Solomon finished his prayer and dedicating the temple, fire came down from heaven and the glory of the Lord filled the temple. So here it is, prayers that went forth were a sweet aroma to God's nostrils regarding Solomon prayer request. The prayers of the righteous availeth much power. So we find out that God responded to Solomon prayer publicly by releasing and manifesting fire from heaven which consumed the burnt offering, sacrifice, and the glory of the lord filled the temple. You see Jesus had not arrived yet so according to the customs of the Old Testament people had to offer animal sacrifices as part of the blood covenant.

This cleansing of sin by the blood prepared the way spiritually for the fire and glory to come down. Keeping the fire burning in a believers lifestyle will always require some form of sacrifice. Sacrifice means to give up something, let go of something or surrender. We should willingly sacrifice unto God out of love and relationship.

The Sacrifice in Romans 12:1, states I beseech you therefore, brethren, by the mercies of God, that you present your bodies a living sacrifice, holy, acceptable to God which is our reasonable service. What does it mean to be a living sacrifice? It means a believer allows his or herself to die to their own fleshly desires and wants that are outside the will of God, this creates access for the Christian to become transformed through the Word of God and by the fire of the Holy Ghost. After all a believer who practices a lifestyle of being a living sacrifice is proof that the word is actively working in their life. Dying to self-cause believers to receive correction and reproof from leaders, humbly submit, inwardly as well as outwardly, finding no rebellion or resentment rising up within the heart. When dying to self we can see our brothers and sister prosper without being envious. When dying to self a person can celebrate honestly when others receive breakthroughs knowing that he or she is next in line for a miracle. When dying to self a believer refuses to let anger rise in the heart or even defend self, but take it all in patiently. When keeping the fire burning we learn how to sacrifice and we discover how to suffer. Suffering can be described as one who is in pain or distress. James 5:11 says My brethren, take the prophets, who spoke in the name of the Lord, as an example of suffering and patience. Indeed we count them blessed who endure. We have heard of the perseverance of Job and seen the end intended by the Lord that reveals how compassionate and merciful he is toward believers. The tender mercies of God make an abundant mends for all of our sufferings and afflictions. Let us serve our God and endure our trials, as those who believe at the end God will crown all. Romans 8:18 says For I consider that the sufferings of this present time are not worthy to be compared to the glory which shall be revealed in us. Nevertheless, when we suffer with Christ we will be glorified with him. The sufferings of the saints in this present time cannot compare with the glory that God is going to expose through our story called life. So for this very reason we should willingly pay the price and suffer for righteousness sake. As believers our lives are like a movie playing backwards to the beginning and when it's time for God to unveil his master piece to the world they will know there is a God in heaven because of the sanctification process called the refining fire. The suffering is short and light according to 2 Cor.4:17. For our light affliction, which is but for a moment, worketh for us a far more exceeding and eternal weight of glory. However, the weight of Glory that will be revealed will leave us with joy unspeakable joy from the work that God has done inside and revealing it on the outside. See no one can measure the weight of glory for it is rich and great. In other words there is a blessing in

suffering for righteousness. Keeping the fire burning

teaches us how to sacrifice, suffer, and understand how to

be set apart. Oh! Yes consecration and sanctification are

important ingredients used in the fire. Sanctification is this

life long process. God continually shows and reveals to

every believer as he or she walks through the fire process

called deliverance can be looked at like an onion. This

concept allows the Holy Spirit to refine Christians then

teach them how to make decisions by choosing to do what

is right according to the Word of God. This process can be

difficult at times but it is so worth it, because at the same

time we grow to know Jesus more closely and intimately.

God keeps working on us and making us better, but we

won't be perfect until it is time to go to heaven. The  Holy

Spirit lives on the inside of each believer and his job is to mold, shape, and transform us into the kind of holy and righteous people God ordained us to be. 1 Thessalonians 5:23 Now may the God of peace Himself sanctify you completely; and may your whole spirit, soul and body be preserved blameless at the coming of our lord Jesus Christ. God wants to sanctify every believer-body, soul and spirit. This means that through the power of the Holy Spirit and the blood of Jesus Christ he wants to purify and cleanse a person's physical body, thoughts, emotion and spirit. Through the sanctification process God can fill us completely with Himself. When a person is completely filled with Jesus, he is a whole and free person whom God can use. Keeping the fire burning in our temples require sacrifice, suffering, and sanctifying ourselves, we will experience the manifestation of his glory filling the temple just like Solomon did in 1 Chronicles 7: 2  says And the priest could not enter the house of the Lord because the glory of the Lord had filled the Lord's house. When all the children of Israel saw how the fire came down, and the glory of the Lord was on the temple  as they bowed their faces to the ground on the pavement, and worshiped and praised the Lord, saying For he is good, for his mercy endures forever. So the children of the Israel witnessed the fire that came down from glory of the Lord on the temple, as a result they laid before the lord and with reverence adoring the glory of God by expressing their cheerful submission to him because they felt unworthy to be in God presence. This is where we are as children of God, the higher we go into God presence the more we should die, become a living sacrifice and learn to suffer so the Glory of

the Lord will fill our temple physically and spiritually.

When a believer is baptized with the Holy Spirit and fire

the inner temple of the human personality is filled with the

glory of the God, which is the way God designed it from

the beginning. The fire keeps on burning when we stay

connected to God through prayer. The fire keeps on

burning when we seek the face of God. The fire keeps on

burning when we die to self so Christ can live through us.

The fire keeps on burning when we learn how to suffer for

righteousness. The fire keeps on burning when we pray in

the Holy Ghost. Fire is described in Daniel 7:9 the throne,

O Lord is like a fiery flame. See Jer 23:29 Says is not my

word like a fire. Can you here Malachi 3:3 He will sit as a

refiner and a purifier of silver; He will purify the son of

Levi; and purge them as gold and silver that they may offer to the Lord an offering in righteousness. He will purge them as gold and silver, which means he is sanctifying and cleaning us outward and inwardly. The Holy Spirit is working in our life like a consuming fire so we can sincerely be converted and committed to God. Keeping the fire burning should be our lifestyle. Jesus knew about the Holy Ghost and fire. John the Baptist tells us in Mathew 3: 11 that I indeed baptize you with water unto repentance, but He who is coming after me is mightier than I, whose sandals I am not worthy to carry. He will baptize you with the Holy Spirit and fire. The fire will continue to burn within believers as we stay connected to the true vine.

## Chapter 2

## There is a blessing

## Within

## The flame of fire

2 Timothy 1:6, 7 The average Christian would not associate the word "fire" with the Creator Himself. Our first thoughts would probably be Hell-fire, the Lake of Fire, or Sodom and Gomorra. It may be surprising to many Christians that the word "fire," and its attributes of "light" and "heat," speak more of the Creator and His goodness than of a destructive force against His enemies.

Clearly, the writers of the Bible employed the use of fire in many different ways. However, when it came to the spiritual aspect about fire the writers compared fire to the attributes of God. Yahweh manifested Himself in various forms of fire on many different occasions. We find some of these manifestations in the making of the Covenant with

Abraham (Gen. 15:17) the burning bush with Moses (Ex. 3:2-4), pillar of fire with Israel (Ex. 13:21), on Sinai Jesus, John and Peter (Exo.19:18), in the flame on the altar (Judg. 13:20), and Yahweh answering by fire with Elisha (1 Kings 18:24, 38). However, one thing about Fire is that it's never still. It moves. It seeks to consume. This is true whether it be the hateful fire of man's anger or the passion to bring healing, joy, and love to those around us. Fire always produces change. It will force one to act or to respond. Fire brings focus. "Fiery" trials often let us know what kind of fire is burning in our bosom. Fire just stirs up the molecules until they reach a point of agitation great enough for atoms within a molecule to be released from one another. Fire divides. The same thing happened when Jesus sent forth the fire of which He spoke. He sent forth a seed (spark) of faith which broke the power of tradition which held people together to a lower form of government. Jesus fiery word, was released to serve in a higher kingdom, the kingdom of God, where there is righteousness, peace, and joy. There is blessing within the flame. Daniel Chapter 3 tells a story about a blessing in the flame. Nebuchadnezzar was a supreme egomaniac. He made a giant gold statue of himself, and he commanded everyone in his kingdom to fall down and worship it. Every time the people heard the sound of the horn, flute, harp, lyre, psaltery, in symphony with all kinds of music they had to bow down and pay homage to the statue. Daniel's three friends refused to fall down and worship the statue of Nebuchadnezzar because if they had done so they would have been worshiping idols and displeasing to God. Shadrach, Meshach and Abednego were arrested for refusing to worship the king. Daniels three friends went against the flow and made a decision to ignore the peer pressure and comments of others instead they made a decision to obey God. How many people understand that believers can't please everyone? How many understand that somebody is always going to have a problem with what another person does whether it is good or bad?

People sometime allow themselves to be use by Satan. Satan an accuser of the brethren. Rev 12:10:11 describes those who overcame the accuser of our brethren, the devil as those who were overcome him by the blood of the Lamb and by the word of their testimony. The three Hebrew boys did not love their lives to death. What is it that your family and friends are expecting you to compromise to please them over God? Some refuse to attend church on Sunday, going to the bars and washing cars instead of being in the house of the Lord. However, only God is worthy of our worship. How will you respond to the blessing in the flame? Daniel and his friends provide us with the model for a faithful testimony under the threat of torture and death. Daniel and his friends remained faithful to God while in King Nebuchadnezzar's court.  When there was an order in the land to worship the image of gold. Daniel and his friends refused to bow down and worship anything but the true and living God. Under extreme pressure and even under the threat of death, these loyal men of God would not compromise their faith. Because of this they were sentenced to death by King Nebuchadnezzar and ordered to be burned alive in a fiery furnace. How far would you be willing to go to hang on to your commitment and loyalty to God? When we are under fire our victory will be determined on how we respond to life challenges. Daniel's friends were thrown into a superhot blazing furnace but they were supernaturally delivered by God. The God to whom they were faithful was faithful to them and they were able to walk around in burning flames, without being harmed. In addition, the fourth man looked like the Son of God who mysteriously appeared with them in the furnace and walked with them in the middle of the fire. Yes there is a blessing in the flame. God did not only give them personal protection but he was faithful to them. Since they were willing to suffer for their testimony, but this fourth man who was a theophany of preincarnate manifestation of Jesus Christ the Messiah appeared among them. Needlesstosay, Nebuchadnezzar and his assistants were amazed by the whole thing and not only gave glory to the true God, but passed new laws to protect Daniel and his friends. There is a blessing in the flame so instead of hating the trial embrace it because during the consuming fire, it's process will lead you to grow and mature in the word of God.

## Chapter 3

## Burn baby Burn

Ezekiel 20:47, 48

As we hear the word burn baby burn we automatically think of something being set on fire. In the Bible most of the time fire represents God presence and power. As previously mentioned when we hear the word fire we automatically visualize something hot. The word "fire, has attributes of "light" and "heat," that speak more of the Creator and His goodness than of a destructive force against His enemies. Burn baby burn is an indication that something needs to die in the life of a believer by the fire of the Holy Ghost. As we look at the book of Ezekiel. Ezekiel was warning the people what was about to happen to them. As we look at the previous verses the Israelites were worshipping idols and giving gifts to God at the same time. How many know we cannot serve two masters either we going to hate one and love other. They did not believe that their God was the one and true God instead they worshiped him and other Gods of the land. Perhaps they enjoyed the immoral pleasures of idol worshipping. Perhaps they didn't want to miss out on the benefits the idol worshipping would give them. On the other hand they were holding on to their idols of money, power, and pleasure of life. So we have people who are double minded going back and forth and forth and back. How many know that God wants all of our devotion? He will not share his glory with another because he is a jealous God. As we look at our text Ez 20:47 Say to the southern forest: (refers to Jerusalem and Judah) Hear the Word of the Lord. This is what the Sovereign Lord says. Wait a minute lets define Sovereign. Ps 103:19 the Lord has established His throne in the heavens; and His sovereignty rules over all.

Sovereign means dominion, power and authority. How many know that God has unlimited power. God sovereign power has control over all affairs. Dan 7:27 then sovereignty, power and the greatness of the kingdoms under the whole heaven will be handed over to the saints the people of the Most High. His kingdom will be an everlasting kingdom and all the dominions shall serve and obey Him. The Bible declares that God is working out His sovereign plan of redemption for the world and that conclusion is certain. He does not have any doubt about the end results, which take us back to our text. Our Sovereign Lord says I am about to set fire to you and it will consume all your trees both green and dry. The blazing flame will not be quenched, and every face from south to north will be scorched by it. Everyone will see that I the Lord have kindled it and will not be quenching. (this fire will not be put out)Burn baby burn. What I love about God he will never leave us or forsake us. Isaiah 43:2 When thou passest through the waters, I will be with thee; (Just like he was with Moses when they were crossing the red sea and Just like Joshua when they were crossing over Jordan, he will be with you and me) and through the rivers, they shall not overflow thee: when thou walkest through the fire, thou shalt not be burned; neither shall the flame kindle upon thee. Going through rivers of difficulty will either cause us to drown or force us to grow up and mature in the principles of God. If we go in our own strength we are more likely to drown. If we invite the Lord to go with us he will provide protection for us. Burn baby burn. Well I believe that we are in an hour where God is unveiling his glory more to the saints. God came onto the scene to honor His covenant or agreement with Abraham to deliver His people from the cruel taskmasters. He had a better idea for their lives, which was to deliver them and take them to the Promised land. The message here is that God does not want His people to work as slaves in the world system and to be in bondage to sin. How are believers going to be delivered? Moses foreshadowed Christ, who was the ultimate deliverer and who set God's people free from the bondage of slavery to the world system of which Satan is the present ruler. God choose you and me to go forth and set his people free by the power of the Holy Spirit and the blood of the lamb. Burn baby burn. The word said the people were going to be set on fire but it will not consume us. That is accomplished by the Word of God and the Sweet Holy Spirit Roman: 8: 3-4 demonstrates this fact it says For what the law was powerless to do because it was weakened by the flesh, God did send his only Son to be a sin offering. In order that the righteous requirement of the law might be fully met in us, who do not live according to the flesh but according to the Spirit. Jesus gave himself as a sacrifice (sin offering). In the Old Testament times, animal sacrifices were continually offered at the temple. The sacrifices showed the Israelites the seriousness of sin; blood had to be shed before sins could be pardoned. But animal's blood could not really remove sins. The sacrifices could only point to Jesus sacrifice which paid the penalty for all sin. Burn baby Burn is concepts that challenge the believer to grow from one level faith to the next demission of glory.

## Chapter 4

## God is Going to Kindle

## The

## Fire and Flame Within Us

Ezk 20:45-49

As we look at the book of Ezekiel he was a man trained in his youth as a priest in Jerusalem. Ezekiel received a vision of God and a call to serve as a prophet among his people. Ezekiel assignment and message was to combine judgment and hope. As we look in Ezekiel 20: 45-49 he had an assignment to preach and prophesy to the north and south which represented Judah and Jerusalem. Judah and Jerusalem had been full of people, as a forest of trees, but empty of fruit. They were not producing anything that held value. God's word prophesies against those who do not bring forth the fruits of righteousness which is given by God through faith in Christ Jesus. Righteous believers agree to do things right according to the Word of God. Romans 3:32 this righteousness from God comes through faith in Jesus Christ to all who believe. In order for God to kindle the flame and fire within us we must have righteousness and the fruit of righteousness operating in our life. Where can one find fruits of righteousness? The fruits which the righteousness brings forth under the influence of divine grace; see trees of righteousness, are filled with the fruits of righteousness by Christ, and have their fruit unto holiness, and their end is everlasting life. The fruit of the righteous is as the fruit of the tree of life; 'Proverbs 11:30 righteousness is a tree of life, and he who wins souls is wise. A wise person is a model of meaningful and productive living. Like a tree attracts people to shade, his or her sense of purpose attracts others who want to know how they too can find true meaning for life. Ezekiel's assignment was to warn the people about what was getting ready to happen to them because of their disobedience and the lifestyle of serving idol Gods. Because of this kind of behavior God was coming to devour every green tree and every dry tree in them. The blazing flame could not be put out and everyone was going to see that I the Lord have kindled this flame that can't be quenched. Kindling a flame within requires the righteousness of God that strikes the fire to keep the torch within lit bright and shining. So what kind of fruits is being produced in the lifestyle of believers today? Philippians 1:11 gives the answer to being filled with the fruit of righteousness, which is Christ Jesus, unto glory and praise of God. The fruit of righteousness includes all the characteristics and moral traits flowing from a right relationship with God. There is no other way for us to gain fruits of righteousness other than through Christ. Believers filled with the fruit of righteousness are revealed through the attributes and behavior patterns that flow through the heart. The fruits should be seen in the character and lifestyle of believers; and those fruits are in Galatians 5:22, 23 reveals the fruit of the Spirit that is in Jesus Christ but the fruit of the Spirit is love, joy, peace, longsuffering, kindness, goodness, faithfulness, gentleness, self-control, again such there is no law. Being filled with the Spirit causes believers to have balance in character, anointing and charismatic activity. The Holy Spirit's fruit is to be manifested in our lives every bit as much as His gifts are to be shown through us. It is dangerous to give attention to the gifts of the Spirit without being attentive to the fruit of the Spirit. If love is not the driving force behind every gift of the believers then the gifts will have no value. The apostle Paul wanted the believers to show righteousness by living out the Word of God in our everyday life. He commissioned them to do it unto the glory and praise to God. God is being honored when we work under his grace thus appears to men in the fruits of righteousness; and then God is praised by all his work that appears through us. Every genuine follower of God has his glory in view by all that he or she does, says, or intends. As believers we should love to glorify God. Glorifying God shows forth as believers love and walk in obedience to the word of God. This produces the conversion and transformation done in our lives which reveals his glorious power manifesting inside and outside of us. Kindling the flame within requires the fruit of the Spirit operating in our Character. Christians operating without the fruit of the Spirit in his or her lifestyle are spiritually dead with a mind-set that is unaware of the value to produce godly fruit. Kindling the flame and releasing fresh fire within us should be our daily commitment to God. Kindle mean to build or fuel (a fire). b. To set fire to; ignite. 2. To cause to glow; light up: Does anybody need a light called the Holy Ghost Fire? What does God use to set us on fire? Trials and tribulations. What does trials and tribulations produce? Godly character that stretch the believer's faith in God. We also need to celebrate the fiery trials by rejoicing in our sufferings because there is a reward on the other side of the trial and tribulation. Romans 5:3-4 Knowing that tribulation produces perseverance, perseverance character, and character hope. When we move forward during our trials in spite of the situation it proves our faith in God. When a fire and flame is kindling within there shall be some proof of God presence. Jeremiah 20:9 But if I say, "I will not mention him or speak any more in his name," his word is in my heart like a fire, a fire shut up in my bones. I am weary of holding it in; indeed, I cannot. When the fire and flames begin to kindle within we have to tell somebody Jeremiah 23; 29 Is not my word like fire," declares the LORD, "and like a hammer that breaks a rock in pieces? That same fire and power lies within the believers waiting to be lit. John told us he will baptize with water but Jesus came to Baptize with water and fire. When we have opposition on the outside we have to know that the Holy Ghost is doing a work on the inside by kindling the flame and fire within. When we have fire there must be some fuel to kindle a flame. Ps 39:3 My heart grew hot within me, and as I meditated, the fire burned; then I spoke with my tongue. The fire of God kindles within us when we meditate on the Word of God. God is putting a flame and fire within us like he did for the Disciples. Luke 24:32 says And they said to one another, did not our heart burn within us while He talked with us on the road, and while He opened the Scriptures to us. Jesus reveals himself to them through his presence and the Word. Kindling a flame within happens when we walk, commune and spend time with Christ. Believers who seek the face of God can create a fire that lite a torch in our hearts that creates a burning flame on the inside. The more we walk, commune and spend time with the Lord he will reveal things about our life that need to be burned away. When we do things God's way we can make declaration that produce results that will release fresh fire. How do we release fresh fire? By beckoning God presence in our atmosphere releases the consuming fire of God to manifest. That means we are inviting him into our life and situation. Beckon to mean signal with the hand or nod.

When we worship God we are saying come on in the room. Hebrew 12:29 says for God is a Consuming fire. Deuteronomy 4:29 For the LORD your God is a consuming fire, a jealous God. No one can quench or put out God fire. As sons and daughters of the most high God we have dominion, power, authority and fire because of our covenant relationship with Jesus Christ. Know that we can command ye me to the Lord. Isaiah 45:11 and 12 Thus saith the LORD, the Holy One of Israel, and his Maker, Ask me of things to come concerning my sons and concerning the work of my hands command ye me. I have made the earth, and created man on it. My hands stretched out the heavens and their entire host I have commanded. He wants us to take Kingdom dominion, authority and command his power in our lives and circumstance. Know that we release fresh fire that kindles within and bring change inside out. Refresh, renew, restore. When fresh fire is released it consumes things out of us that is not of God. His power operates through us by the Holy Spirit.

2 Timothy 1:6 For this reason I remind you to fan into flame the gift of God, which is in you through the laying on of my hands. Fresh fire is released when we activate the gifts that God put in us. Fresh fire is released when we embrace God's presence. In the presence of God is the fullness of joy and whatever we need God can release it in his presence. Give God Glory, Glory to his name, and Glory to his name! Ps. 24:1-4 The earth is the Lords and everything in it, the world and all that live in it. For he founded it upon the seas and established it upon the waters. Who may ascend into the hills of the Lord? He who has clean hands and a pure heart, who does not lift up his soul to an idol or swear by what is false. He will receive the blessing from the Lord and vindication from God his Savior. Ps. 24:7-10 Lift up your heads, O you gates, be lifted up ye everlasting doors and the King of glory shall come in.

Who is the King of Glory? The Lord strong and Mighty the Lord mighty in battle. Lift up your heads O you gates, even lift them up, ye everlasting doors and the King of glory shall come in. Who is the king of Glory the Lord Almighty is the King of Glory! Glory The glory of God releases fresh fire. Why don't you try him today by letting him kindle your flame and Ignite your fire within?

# Resources

**Bibles:**

**Amplified**

**King James**

**Online Resources:**

**Bible.com**

**Dictionary.com**

www.ingramcontent.com/pod-product-compliance
Lightning Source LLC
Chambersburg PA
CBHW061758040426
42447CB00011B/2367